Dear Parent:

Congratulations! Your child is taking the first steps on an exciting journey. The destination? Independent reading!

STEP INTO READING® will help your child get there. The program offers books at five levels that accompany children from their first attempts at reading to reading success. Each step includes fun stories, fiction and nonfiction, and colorful art. There are also Step into Reading Sticker Books, Step into Reading Math Readers, and Step into Reading Phonics Readers—a complete literacy program with something to interest every child.

Learning to Read, Step by Step!

Ready to Read Preschool–Kindergarten
• **big type and easy words** • **rhyme and rhythm** • **picture clues**
For children who know the alphabet and are eager to begin reading.

Reading with Help Preschool–Grade 1
• **basic vocabulary** • **short sentences** • **simple stories**
For children who recognize familiar words and sound out new words with help.

Reading on Your Own Grades 1–3
• **engaging characters** • **easy-to-follow plots** • **popular topics**
For children who are ready to read on their own.

Reading Paragraphs Grades 2–3
• **challenging vocabulary** • **short paragraphs** • **exciting stories**
For newly independent readers who read simple sentences with confidence.

Ready for Chapters Grades 2–4
• **chapters** • **longer paragraphs** • **full-color art**
For children who want to take the plunge into chapter books but still like colorful pictures.

STEP INTO READING® is designed to give every child a successful reading experience. The grade levels are only guides. Children can progress through the steps at their own speed, developing confidence in their reading, no matter what their grade.

Remember, a lifetime love of reading starts with a single step!

Dedicated to the kids of Wyoming. We set up an election for you to choose your favorite dinosaur— and you chose Triceratops!

With thanks to Dr. James Kirkland for his assistance in the preparation of this book.

Text copyright © 2004 by Dr. Robert T. Bakker.
Illustrations copyright © 2004 by Luis V. Rey
All rights reserved under International and Pan-American Copyright Conventions.
Published in the United States by Random House Children's Books,
a division of Random House, Inc., New York, and simultaneously in Canada
by Random House of Canada Limited, Toronto.

www.stepintoreading.com

Educators and librarians, for a variety of teaching tools, visit us at
www.randomhouse.com/teachers

Library of Congress Cataloging-in-Publication Data
Bakker, Robert T.
Maximum Triceratops / by Robert T. Bakker ; illustrated by Luis Rey. — 1st ed.
   p. cm. — (Step into reading. A step 5 book)
SUMMARY: Introduces the very rare—and controversial—*Triceratops maximus,* an aggressive,
herbivorous dinosaur capable of driving off even a *Tyrannosaurus rex.*
ISBN 0-375-82304-2 (trade) — ISBN 0-375-92304-7 (lib. bdg.)
1. Triceratops—Juvenile literature. [1. Triceratops. 2. Dinosaurs.]
I. Rey, Luis, ill. II. Title. III. Series: Step into reading. Step 5 book.
QE862.O65B35 2004 567.915'8—dc21   2003003811

Printed in the United States of America   10 9 8 7 6 5 4 3 2 1   First Edition

STEP INTO READING, RANDOM HOUSE, and the Random House colophon are registered trademarks
of Random House, Inc.

STEP INTO READING®

STEP 5

MAXIMUM
TRICERATOPS

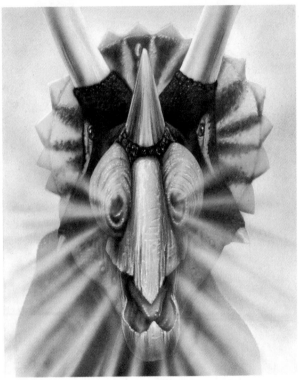

by Dr. Robert T. Bakker
illustrated by Luis V. Rey

Random House 🏠 New York

Chapter One

Tyrannosaurus rex was the biggest, baddest, bone-crunchingest meat-eater of its time, right? And every other dinosaur was afraid of it, right? Wrong! There was one animal that scared even the mighty *T. rex*.

Let's go back in time about 66 million years to what is now the state of Wyoming. It's the very end of the Cretaceous Period. There are no mountains or dry plains like there are today. Instead, there are swamps and lagoons, where wide, slow rivers flow into a shallow ocean. You are a *Tyrannosaurus rex* and you're tracking your favorite prey—a wounded duckbill dino—into a swamp forest.

You splash across a shallow pond and scare some soft-shell turtles. Little furballs shaped like hedgehogs (the ancestors of us humans) squeak and scamper up a tree.

You smell other meat-eaters, too. Raptors. You can't have *them* messing with your duckbill. So you hiss and snarl, and the raptors run across the riverbank, kicking up sand. All the animals are terrified of you, and that feels good.

But then it happens. Your nostrils

twitch. Something's in the air. A musky smell. You stop snarling and forget about the duckbill.

There's a *boom* in the horsetail reeds. You flinch. It's a horrible sound, as deep and loud as a hundred tubas. Instinct—the voice inside your head—screams, *Run! Run away now!*

Your legs start pumping, but it's hard to run. You trip on a clump of ferns. Something as heavy as a bus is plowing through the underbrush, *coming right at you!*

The ground shakes under your feet. The sound is so deep that you feel it in your joints. Your stomach feels funny and your head hurts.

A massive face bursts through the reeds. Two huge, clear red eyes stare sideways behind a long, sharp beak. A seven-foot pointy horn juts out from each eyebrow. The gigantic head swings swiftly back and forth, the horns breaking branches and sending leaves flying. If you're an old *T. rex,* you probably have scars made by horns like these. You dodge left, but the monster is quicker in the turns. You dodge right, but the horned beast is catching up.

The voice in your head yells, *Get out of the swamp! Run to the open meadow!* But it's too late. A horrible pain shoots through your thigh. You've been gored by the monster's horn.

Despite the wound, you break away, smashing through the last 20 yards of swamp. Once you're in the open meadow, you can easily run on your long legs. You're lucky to be alive. Your wound will heal. And you've learned a valuable lesson: never chase a duckbill into a swamp when a giant horned monster is around.

Chapter Two

Who *is* the giant horned swamp monster?
It's not a relative of *T. rex*. It's not
Spinosaurus from the movie *Jurassic Park
III*. In fact, it's not a meat-eater at all. It's a
veggie-saur—a 100 percent plant-eating,
herbivorous dinosaur. The brute who
stabbed *T. rex* is Maximum *Triceratops*!

Movies about dinosaurs sometimes make us think that all meat-eaters were dangerous and all plant-eaters were friendly. But that's wrong. In nature today, the most dangerous critters on land are huge, strong vegetarians. African elephants charge lions and try to squash their cubs. Black rhinos use their long horns to spear hyenas. Hippos use their big teeth to chop crocodiles in half.

Why are the giant plant-eaters so aggressive? Because meat-eaters like to eat

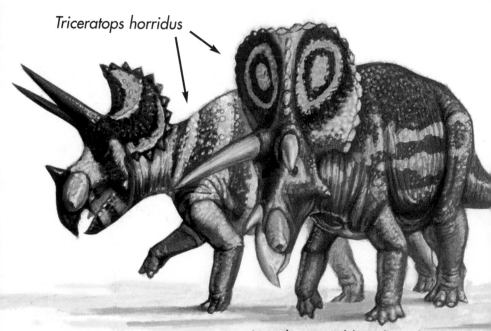

Triceratops horridus

(Another possible color scheme)

baby plant-eaters. So adult plant-eaters try to chase away meat-eaters before they become a serious threat.

Back in the days of *T. rex,* the most aggressive veggie-saur was *Triceratops,* and the most common kind was *Triceratops horridus.* But the most dangerous T'tops was the super-rare, super-huge *Triceratops maximus.* Maximum T'tops is a mighty mystery monster. Bone diggers have been arguing about it for 70 years.

Maximum T'tops

The greatest T'tops fossil hunter of all time was Dr. Barnum Brown, who worked for the American Museum of Natural History in New York City 100 years ago. He found 500 Horrid T'tops skulls while searching the rocks in Montana.

But the one T'tops specimen that Brown *didn't* expect to find was the giant neck he dug in 1933. The size was stunning—it was off the charts. Then scientists rediscovered a super-sized T'tops skull hidden in storage at Yale. The Yale head matched Brown's neck. These two stupendous discoveries—skull and neck—were evidence of a new and super-rare T'tops species, the one Brown named *Triceratops maximus*.

The average Horrid T'tops head is about six feet from nose to back of skull. But this Maximum T'tops head was over eight feet long! It is the heaviest skull of any known dinosaur. In fact, it is the heaviest skull of any land-living animal—*ever!*

blood grooves

But was the big guy *really* a different species? Right after Brown announced his discovery, other scientists said, "Hold on! We don't believe it!" They thought that *Triceratops maximus* was just a freaky Horrid T'tops grown extra, *extra* large. After all, Maximum T'tops was outnumbered 200 to 1 by regular-sized *Triceratops*.

Maybe Maximum T'tops *isn't* a different

"Andre the Giant"—enlarged jaw!

Normal size human

species. But I suspect that Barnum Brown was correct, and I'll tell you why.

Giant members of a species usually have jaws and snouts that are extra thick. Human giants are that way. "Andre the Giant" was a famous wrestler and actor, and he had a really enlarged jaw. But the Maximum T'tops skull looks perfectly normal, except for its size.

Maximum T'tops—
normal jaw

Triceratops horridus—
normal jaw

Plus, we now know that evolution *does* split up giant animals into species of different sizes. Take African elephants, for instance. People used to think all African elephants were the same species. That's what I taught students in my college courses. Sure, we found smaller elephants in deep forests and bigger ones on the plains. But we all thought that forest elephants and plains elephants could interbreed and make healthy baby elephants.

It's embarrassing, but all us scientists turned out to be wrong! Elephant DNA—the stuff genes are made of—was studied carefully in the lab in 2000–2001. And it turned out that the really big plains elephants couldn't breed with the smaller forest ones. There are two *different* species of elephants living in Africa.

Did evolution split *Triceratops* into regular- and super-sized species? How can we tell?

That's a tough question. If they were alive today, you could put a Maximum T'tops and a Horrid T'tops together in a nature preserve and see if they had babies. But that's not possible.

Can we find enough fossil DNA in our *Triceratops* specimens to run tests? Probably not. DNA rots too quickly to become fossilized often.

But here's something we *can* do. When evolution splits animals into two species, they usually live in different habitats. Forest elephants stay in the deep, dark jungles. Big plains elephants prefer drier woods and swamps near plains. We need to dig up more T'tops and study where they lived.

forest elephant

plains elephant

duct tape

Maybe Maximum T'tops preferred different places, away from Horrid T'tops.

Either way, whether Maximum T'tops was a freaky giant Horrid T'tops or a rare species, it was the worst thing a *T. rex* could bump into! Horrid T'tops was as big and strong as an elephant. But Maximum T'tops was as heavy and powerful as *two* elephants duct-taped together!

Maximum T'tops!

Chapter Three

All T'tops heads—the common ones and the super-maxis—are fabulous. Even though both types of skulls were heavy, they were quick and maneuverable. They could be swiveled around in half a second, pointing the horns in any direction.

How could a head do that? Come to the Glenrock Paleontological Museum in Glenrock, Wyoming, where I work, and look at a T'tops skull turned upside down. You'll see the joint where the head attached to the neck. It's a ball joint about the size and shape of a grapefruit.

Ball joints are great for quick movements. You've got a ball joint at your shoulder. That's why you can swing your arm fast in any direction. But ball joints between the head and neck are very rare. This joint would let T'tops flip their heavy skulls much faster than most other dinosaurs.

Rhinos today have heavy horned heads that look a little like T'tops heads. But the joint between the head and neck in a rhino isn't a ball joint. It is a hinge. The rhino can't flip its head around as fast as a T'tops could.

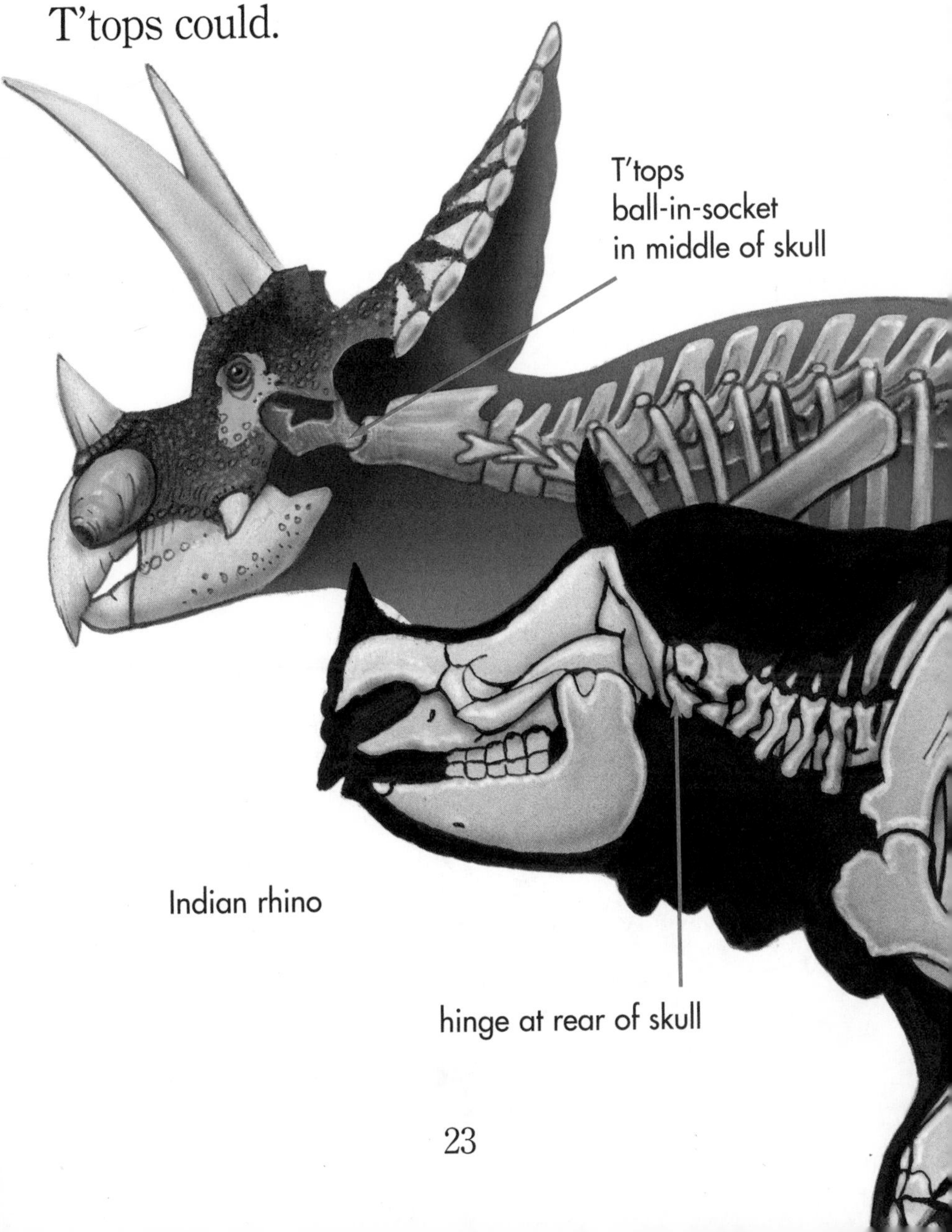

T'tops
ball-in-socket
in middle of skull

Indian rhino

hinge at rear of skull

Triceratops had another trick for moving its head fast—the huge skull was perfectly balanced because the ball joint was right in the middle. In most other horned animals— rhinos, for instance—the neck attaches to the head at the rear. But a *Triceratops* had its joint located exactly halfway from the snout to the back. So a T'tops could twitch its neck muscles just a little bit to the left, and its head would turn left in milliseconds.

These muscles pull sideways.

If the muscles twitched up, the head would instantly swing up.

The balanced *Triceratops* head would be the most dangerous weapon in the Cretaceous Period—*if* T'tops had strong muscles to move the head. Were T'tops neck muscles thick and strong? You bet! Muscles themselves don't fossilize. That's because they rot too quickly after an animal dies. But we can see how big the muscles were when we look at where the muscles attached to the bones.

These muscles pull up.

The muscles that pull the head sideways are attached to a piece of bone that's next to the ball joint. And in T'tops, this piece of bone is wide and thick. That shows the muscles were incredibly strong and could swing the head left or right with great power. The muscles that pull the head up are attached to a bone that's just above the ball joint—and that piece is wide and thick, too. The *Triceratops* horn-jab would be fast and unstoppable.

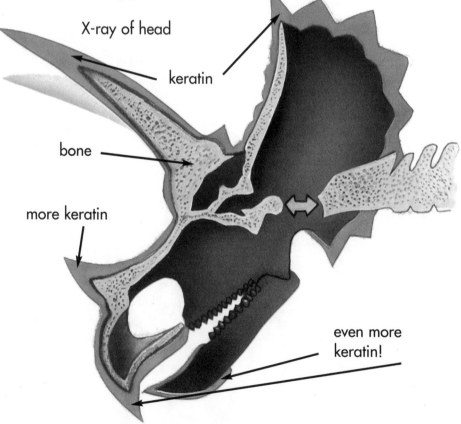

X-ray of head

keratin

bone

more keratin

even more keratin!

Chapter Four

What about those horns? Could they break
if a T'tops rammed another dinosaur? Bone
by itself is brittle and can crack and get
infected. To make a strong horn, you must
do what a buffalo does—grow one made
from two parts. Grow bone on the inside and
a protective layer of fingernail-like skin,
called keratin, on the outside. That kind of
horn is nearly unbreakable. Did T'tops have
two-part horns?

Well, keratin usually rots so fast after a critter dies that it doesn't fossilize. But we can tell how thick the keratin layer was by looking at blood grooves on the bone. Keratin keeps growing throughout an animal's life. So the horn needs arteries to bring blood to grow the layer. The bone in a buffalo horn has lots of grooves on it for arteries. If you find fossil horns with lots of grooves, that proves the keratin layer was thick.

Did T'tops have keratin layers to reinforce the horn? Absolutely. *Triceratops* horns are covered with grooves—deep ones—for big arteries. The keratin was especially thick and strong. A T'tops horn could stab a *T. rex* right through the rib cage and not suffer damage.

T'tops also had another weapon. It could bite hard. The beak at the front of its mouth was hooked like a snapping turtle's. And there was an outer layer of keratin here, too.

A big snapping turtle can bite through a wooden spoon. T'tops could bite through a *T. rex* shin just as easily as it could bite through a tree.

Ouch!

Triceratops horridus and *Triceratops maximus* weren't just well armed, they were well *armored,* too—at their most vulnerable spot, the neck. Most predators bite their victims at the neck. Cats and wolves and weasels are born with the instinct to bite their prey hard, just behind the head. If a *T. rex* bit the neck of a T'tops, the T'tops would die instantly. But *T. rex* couldn't *get at* the neck of a *Triceratops!* There was a layer of armor in the way.

Look at the T'tops head behind the eye sockets. There's a wide flare of bone that covers the entire neck. And the bone is very thick, with many grooves. That means the flare of bone was covered with thick, hard keratin. In fact, nearly the entire face was covered with keratin. And all around the edge of the neck armor are sharp little horns, like the teeth on a buzz saw. If a rex bit the little horns, it would cut its mouth.

Ouch! Ouch!

A Horrid T'tops had such a deadly head, a *T. rex* would have to be very careful and clever to kill one. But to successfully attack a *Triceratops maximus,* a *T. rex* would have to be even more clever and careful . . . and a little bit nuts.

Chapter Five

A T'tops head not only *looks* scary, it would *sound* scary, too. The holes in the bone for the nostrils are huge. This extra-large hole works like an echo chamber to amplify sound. Horses have echo chamber–like nostrils in their skulls, and that's why horse snorts are louder than cow snorts.

Triceratops was a super-snorter. The big holes in the snout would make nose noises extra loud. Loud snorts from a big animal like *Triceratops* can be used to communicate by infra-sound, or noise so deep that it makes the ground shake.

Rhinos and elephants and alligators make infra-sounds that pass through soil, rocks, trees, and even buildings. Infra-sounds can travel farther through the ground than normal sounds travel through the air! Elephants can call to each other from miles away by making the earth shake.

But elephants don't use their ears to hear infra-sounds. They use their feet. The big pads on an elephant's sole are spongy and vibrate when other elephants send infra-sound messages. The pads on T'tops' feet were also spongy enough to detect vibrations.

Loud, deep sounds can also be used as close-range weapons. I once stood too close to an African elephant when it "trumpeted," or made an angry, loud noise. The ground shook and I almost fell over! Deep, infra-sound noises hurt your brain and upset your sense of balance. If a *T. rex* got too close to a big *Triceratops,* the T'tops might blow its nose so loud that the rex would get dizzy.

Chapter Six

Triceratops was shaped a lot like a rhino: the body was round and low, and the legs were bent at the elbow and knee. Today, in the wet forests of Asia, rhinos bash their way through the brush and make tunnels in the jungle. *Triceratops* probably moved like a battering ram, too.

Rhinos can turn on a dime. Could T'tops do that? To turn fast, you need big feet so you don't slip—especially if the ground is muddy. We know T'tops liked mud because we find its bones in rocks that have black layers made from swamps full of rotten leaves.

Take a look at T'tops' feet. They're like extra-wide snow tires. The hind feet have four big toes and fossil footprints show they had big pads. The front feet had five toes and medium-sized pads. These big, padded feet would spread T'tops' body weight and help grip muddy ground.

People who go to horse races have a name for horses who are good at running on wet, swampy ground. They call them "mudders." Mom T'tops was a mudder, Dad T'tops was a mudder, and all their little babies were mudders, too.

Chapter Seven

When *Triceratops* roamed over Wyoming, there were other dinosaurs around who were not mudders. The most common veggie-saur was the duckbill dino called *Edmontosaurus* (named for the Canadian city with a great hockey team where it was first discovered). Edmontosaurs can get pretty big—almost as heavy as a common T'tops. But duckbills had small feet. Their hind paws had only three short toes and the front paws had four thin toes with tiny pads.

duckbill—small paws   T'tops (mudder!)—big paws

Duckbills couldn't turn as fast on mud as a T'tops. So we had a hunch that duckbills avoided swampy places. To figure out if this hunch was right, the museum in Glenrock took a dinosaur census—we counted all the dinosaurs found in a half dozen valleys.

If T'tops and duckbills didn't live in the same habitats, they shouldn't be fossilized in the same places. There's one valley in Wyoming where we found two dozen spots with T'tops bones. But we found only one duckbill.

In other valleys in Wyoming, nearly all the fossils are duckbills, and we didn't find *any* T'tops. So it looks like our hunch was right. T'tops liked squishy soil and duckbills liked it hard.

Chapter Eight

A lot of books show T'tops in big herds, with the adults standing in a circle protecting their babies in the middle. I think that's wrong—and here's why.

Any extinct species that lived in big herds should have left its skeletons in big heaps—at least sometimes. That's because herds sometimes die together in a drought or flood. African antelopes called gnus die that way. Sometimes hundreds of gnus drown while crossing a river and get buried in sandbars. That's bad news for gnus, but good news for crocodiles *and* future paleontologists!

Did T'tops die in piles? Their earlier, smaller relatives did. One-horned dinos

Did T'tops live in herds?

called centrosaurs were buried in giant bone beds with dozens and dozens of skeletons. So were the spike-collared dinos called styracosaurs. Duckbills are found in immense bone beds with *hundreds* of skeletons. But not T'tops. We've never found more than two or three in any one spot. So it looks like T'tops wasn't like its close relations. It didn't like crowds.

We've got a similar situation today with rhinos. The white rhino likes to live in groups. But its close cousin, the black rhino, is a loner.

Nope. It was a loner.

Did Maximum T'tops fight the regular-sized Horrid T'tops? Probably yes. Big herbivores *do* fight with each other. During dry African summers, elephants chase black rhinos away from water holes and white rhinos sometimes chase elephants. In India, bull rhinos use their horns and teeth to kill elephants who get too close to their breeding grounds.

There must have been times when a family of *Triceratops horridus* battled a great bull Maximum T'tops. It's something I'd love to see and hear—trees must have been uprooted and bushes trampled, and all the other dinos must have run for cover to escape the ear-splitting din.

growing up

just hatched

full-grown

Chapter Nine

There are still unsolved mysteries about Maximum T'tops. If being super-sized made you meaner and tougher to kill, why didn't all T'tops grow to maximum dimensions?

Maybe that's because there's a downside to being a giant—it takes a long time to grow up and find a mate and make babies. Maximum T'tops would take longer to grow into an adult than would regular-sized *Triceratops*. So after hundreds and thousands and millions of years, the common T'tops would produce many more eggs, which would grow up into many more common *Triceratops*.

And that brings us back to furballs. Remember the hedgehog-like animals at the beginning of this story? They're mammals—warm-blooded and smart little human relatives who were evolving fast when T'tops ruled the vegetarian way of life. Furballs ate fruit and berries and nuts, and so competed with the big horned dinosaurs.

Of course, a T'tops could squash a little mammal with one swipe of its paw. But the furballs had a way of fighting back: they bred like rabbits. Faster, even.

A T'tops needed at least six years to grow up and become a mom. A baby furball, however, could grow up in just six months. And a furball could have children, and grandchildren, and great-great-great-great-great-great-great-great-great-great-grandchildren before a baby T'tops could grow up and have her first kid.

In the Cretaceous Period, furballs were breeding machines. And when the dinosaurs died out, these mammalian ancestors kept on breeding and evolving . . . and eventually split up into thousands of species, including dogs and cats and cows and humans.

I admire Maximum T'tops. It was surrounded by enemies big and small, yet it survived until the very end of the Age of

Dinosaurs. In a one-on-one battle, no dinosaur was deadlier. So the next time you're arguing about who was the most dangerous dino, don't say *Tyrannosaurus rex*! In a lot of ways, that's a wrong answer.

If we took a time-traveling school bus back to the Cretaceous Period, the dinosaur most likely to ram the bus and knock it over would be *Triceratops maximus*.

If Maximum T'tops were smart enough to plaster a bumper sticker on its wide rear end, the sticker would say:

VEGGIE-SAURS RULE!